PREDATOR VS PREY

HOW SNAKES

AND OTHER REPTILES

ATTACK

TIM HARRIS

WAYLAND
www.waylandbooks.co.uk

First published in Great Britain in 2021 by Wayland
Copyright © Hodder and Stoughton, 2021
All rights reserved.

HB ISBN: 978 1 5263 1455 0
PB ISBN: 978 1 5263 1456 7

Printed and bound in China

Editor: Amy Pimperton
Design: www.smartdesignstudio.co.uk
Picture research: Diana Morris

Picture credits:
Dreamstime: Denis Jacobsen 9b; Pritasdee Jaipinta 17t, 30; Matthjis Kuijpers 23r; **iStock**:Tegmen 19t. **Nature PL**: Guy Edwardes back cover r, 13t; Daniel Heuclin 11t, 21b; Chien Lee/Minden 3c, 22, 23t; Chris Mattison 24, 31; Pete Oxford 12. **Shutterstock**: Abdulalimas 21cr; Artur Balytsky 23c; Been there YB 21t; BlueRing Media 29c; Rvan M Bolton back cover c, 27b; Buteo 9t; Patrik K Campbell 8; EcoPrint back cover l, 6; Fivespots 20; Frantisekhojdysz 5c; GolF2532 14; Ken Griffiths 5b; Andrey Gudkov 15b; Tobias Hauke 25t; Lorraine Hudgins front cover c; Eric isselee 15t,18, 27t; Anna Kucherova frotn cover tr, 2c, 19br; Jeroen Langeveld 1r, 4bl; Martin Lukac 16; LynxVector 29bl; Macrovector 25cr; Maquiladora 7cr, 13cr,15cl ,17cl, 27cr; Nadya Art 9cr, 15cr, 19c, 19bl; Pan stock 29t; Peterpancake 7t; Bambang Prihnawan 27cl; Pumbastyle 1c, 5t; Janos Rautonen front cover tl; Reptiles4all 1l, 4c, 7b, 10, 11b, 25b, 26; Robuart 9cl; Rvector 25cl; Sarunrod 23bl; SaveJungle 11cl; Yuri Schmidt 13cl; Shanvood 21cl; Spreadthedesign 17cr; Alex Stemmer 2l,13b; VectorShow 7cl, 11cr; Sista Vongjintanaruks 2r, 4br; Wet Lizard Photography 3l, 28; Wild and free naturephoto 29br; Danny Ye 3r, 17b.

Wayland, an imprint of
Hachette Children's Group
Part of Hodder and Stoughton
Carmelite House
50 Victoria Embankment
London EC4Y 0DZ

An Hachette UK Company
www.hachettechildrens.co.uk
www.hachette.co.uk

CONTENTS

REPTILE PREDATORS

Reptiles are an incredibly varied group of animals. Snakes, lizards, crocodiles and turtles are all types of reptile. All reptiles are cold-blooded. This means that their bodies can't make their own warmth. Instead they rely on the heat in the air around them to warm up their bodies so that they can move. All reptiles have skin covered in scales or bony plates, or a combination of the two.

Some reptiles, such as the green iguana, are herbivores – they only eat plants. Many more reptiles are predators and carnivores – they hunt and eat other animals. All snakes are carnivores.

Many reptiles, including lots of snakes, are venomous. One of the deadliest is the black mamba. This aggressive snake strikes repeatedly when attacking. It gets its name from the blue-black inside of its mouth. Non-venomous reptiles might use massive power, speed or cunning to trap prey.

BLACK MAMBA

GREEN IGUANA

SNAPPING TURTLE

NILE CROCODILE

Some reptiles live on land while others live in water. Snakes live on every continent except Antarctica and they are adapted to live in their varied habitats. Sea snakes have flat, paddle-shaped tails that help them to swim after ocean prey.

Sidewinding snakes, such as the Peringuey's adder, move sideways across deserts. It is easier for them to move across their loose, sandy habitats in this way, rather than slithering forwards.

PERINGUEY'S ADDER

BANDED SEA KRAIT

Some of the most feared animals on Earth are reptiles. This book uncovers the incredible ways some of these amazing animals hunt to stay alive. From crocodiles lurking in murky waters, to green anacondas squeezing the life out of their victims, read on to find out more.

PUFF ADDER
vs BULLFROG: AMBUSH

Puff adders are deadly snakes that live in savannah – or tropical grassland – in Africa. Their straw-yellow or brown colour helps them to stay hidden during the day. They do most of their hunting at night. Puff adders have very long fangs. Through these, they inject venom deep into their prey. Their venom is strong enough to kill a person.

AMBUSH PREDATOR

Some snakes are constantly on the move in search of their next meal; this is called foraging. A puff adder behaves differently. It tastes the air with its tongue, trying to pick up the scent of other animals. If the snake finds an area that small creatures like to use, it lies in wait, camouflaged and perfectly still. It is an ambush predator – it only attacks when a mouse, lizard or frog comes close.

PATTERNED SCALES FOR CAMOUFLAGE HELP IT BLEND INTO ITS SAVANNAH HABITAT

STRONG VENOM

VERY LONG FANGS AND POWERFUL BITE – SMALLER ANIMALS MAY DIE FROM BEING BITTEN BEFORE THE VENOM HAS TAKEN EFFECT

PATIENT – CAN LIE STILL FOR LONG PERIODS OF TIME

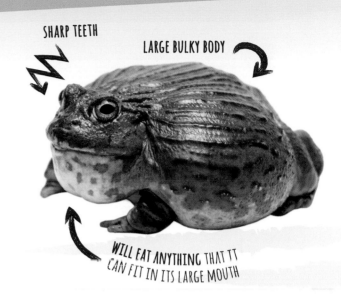

SHARP TEETH

LARGE BULKY BODY

WILL EAT ANYTHING THAT IT CAN FIT IN ITS LARGE MOUTH

AFRICAN BULLFROG

These frogs are active only when the rains come to the African savannah. The rest of the time they hibernate in burrows in the ground. They are some of the world's biggest frogs – and are very aggressive. They eat any animal they come across that they can overpower and fit into their huge mouth. They even swallow small snakes and other frogs. But if a bullfrog gets too close to a puff adder, it might end up inside the snake's mouth!

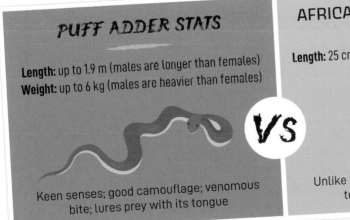

PUFF ADDER STATS

Length: up to 1.9 m (males are longer than females)
Weight: up to 6 kg (males are heavier than females)

AFRICAN BULLFROG STATS

Length: 25 cm (males are larger than females)
Weight: 1.4 kg

Keen senses; good camouflage; venomous bite; lures prey with its tongue

Unlike most frogs it has large, sharp teeth; aggressive; strong

LURE:
TO TEMPT AN ANIMAL TO DO SOMETHING

TONGUE LURE

A puff adder has a special trick to lure a frog closer. It sticks out its tongue and wiggles it around, making it look like a worm. The adder keeps the rest of its body dead still. The frog comes close, thinking it has got itself a bite to eat and – snap! In the blink of an eye, the snake grabs its prey. The strange thing is, puff adders only play this trick on frogs – not mammals or lizards.

GREEN ANACONDA
vs CAPYBARA: CONSTRICTION

The true giant of the snake world, the green anaconda lives in South American swamps and slow-flowing rivers. It is the world's heaviest snake and one of the longest. The biggest anacondas are as long as a school bus. These semi-aquatic reptiles are very much at home in water and are incredibly strong. They hunt pretty much any animal they come across: birds, fish, caimans, mammals as big as deer and giant rodents called capybaras.

SQUEEZED TO DEATH

Unlike many snakes, a green anaconda does not kill with venom. Instead, it approaches silently in the water, grabs prey with sharp, curved teeth and coils its body around its prey. Then it squeezes (constricts) the life out of its victim – or drowns it. An anaconda's jaws open incredibly wide, so the snake swallows its meal whole. After a large meal, the anaconda won't need to eat again for several weeks.

SEMI-AQUATIC: SOMETHING THAT LIVES PARTLY ON LAND AND PARTLY IN WATER

EYES AND NOSTRILS LOCATED ON THE TOP OF THE HEAD

SCALE COLOUR AND PATTERN CAMOUFLAGE ANACONDAS IN AQUATIC VEGETATION

POWERFUL, LONG AND MUSCULAR BODY

CAPYBARA

Capybaras spend much of their time in fresh water where they wallow to keep cool and eat aquatic vegetation. They are the world's largest rodents. An adult capybara weighs as much as an anaconda. These mammals' webbed feet help them to swim well and they can spend up to five minutes underwater.

EYES NEAR THE TOP OF THE HEAD TO SEE WHILE SWIMMING

FUR THAT DRIES OUT QUICKLY

WEBBED FEET

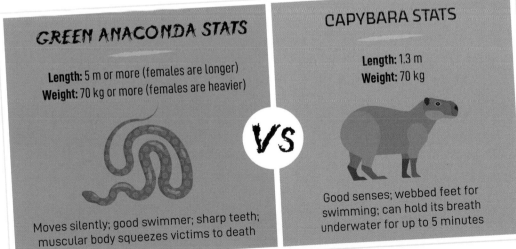

GREEN ANACONDA STATS

Length: 5 m or more (females are longer)
Weight: 70 kg or more (females are heavier)

VS

Moves silently; good swimmer; sharp teeth; muscular body squeezes victims to death

CAPYBARA STATS

Length: 1.3 m
Weight: 70 kg

Good senses; webbed feet for swimming; can hold its breath underwater for up to 5 minutes

SWIMMING KILLERS

Anacondas are agile swimmers. Their eyes and nostrils are near the top of their head so they can remain nearly submerged. And they can hold their breath underwater for up to five minutes.

KING COBRA
VS **INDIAN COBRA: VENOM**

King cobras are the longest of the venomous snakes. Some may grow even longer than green anacondas (see pages 8–9). Though they hunt during the day, they are shy snakes and are rarely seen by people. If threatened, a king cobra lifts the front part of its body upright to confront the threat. It spreads a hood of skin so that it looks even bigger and hisses a warning.

FANGS OF DEATH

Behind this threat, there is real menace. King cobras are highly venomous. One bite delivers 420 milligrams of neurotoxin (poison) through their fangs. This might not sound like a lot, but it is enough to kill 20 people or an elephant. These snakes mostly eat other snakes, including other venomous ones, such as Indian cobras.

EXCELLENT EYESIGHT

INCREDIBLY TOXIC VENOM

HOOD MAKES THE SNAKE LOOK EVEN BIGGER

FLEXIBLE RIBS IN THE NECK ALLOW IT TO EXPAND ITS HOOD

SENSES VIBRATIONS WITH ITS BODY TO HELP IT TRACK PREY

DISTINCTIVE 'SPECTACLE' MARKINGS ON THE HOOD

HIGHLY VENOMOUS, IT IS ONE OF INDIA'S MOST DANGEROUS SNAKES TO HUMANS

INDIAN COBRA

Indian, or spectacled, cobras behave like king cobras in many ways. They hunt other animals, including smaller snakes, which they bite and paralyse with venom. And they also have a hood, which has dark 'spectacle' markings on the back. But Indian cobras are smaller than king cobras – and hungry king cobras have been known to kill Indian cobras, swallowing them whole.

FANG:
A SHARP TOOTH

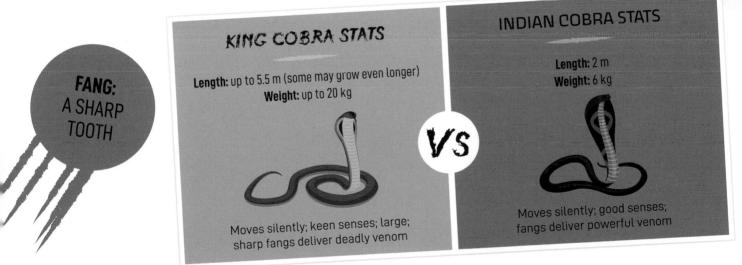

KING COBRA STATS

Length: up to 5.5 m (some may grow even longer)
Weight: up to 20 kg

Moves silently; keen senses; large; sharp fangs deliver deadly venom

VS

INDIAN COBRA STATS

Length: 2 m
Weight: 6 kg

Moves silently; good senses; fangs deliver powerful venom

GROWL OR HISS?

Hissing is a familiar warning sound associated with snakes. Cobras have a very low-pitched hiss that has been described as more like a growl. A hiss is produced in a tube-shaped organ called the glottis. The snake forces air over cartilage in the glottis and this makes the hissing sound

A FOREST COBRA DISPLAYS THE GLOTTIS THAT LIES ON THE BOTTOM OF ITS MOUTH.

EMERALD TREE BOA
VS GLASS FROG: HEAT

An emerald tree boa is almost invisible during the day. It remains motionless on a branch, with its head hidden in the middle of its coils. The snake is bright, emerald green, with a pattern of silvery 'lightning marks' – a camouflage colour scheme that helps it to remain hidden among the foliage of South American rainforests. Emerald tree boas are neither venomous nor especially big, but they have their own special ways of tracking prey.

HEAT-SENSORS

When night falls, emerald tree boas wake up and go hunting. These snakes ambush frogs, lizards and small mammals that are active after dark. The snakes have special organs called heat pits that can 'see' the warmth given off by other animals. And their eyes can detect movement when there is very little light.

If a frog hops beneath a boa's perch, the snake coils its tail around a branch and reaches down to grab its victim. Sharp teeth make sure the prey doesn't escape, then the snake squeezes it to death.

HEAT-SENSITIVE PITS FOR DETECTING PREY

VERTICAL PUPILS TO JUDGE DISTANCE ACCURATELY

MUSCULAR BODY FOR SQUEEZING PREY UNTIL IT SUFFOCATES

SHARP TEETH

CAMOUFLAGE SCALE PATTERN

GLASS FROG

Glass frogs are bright green above, but have see-through skin on the belly – which means the heart and other organs can be seen! Like emerald tree boas, they are predators. They go in search of food – insects and spiders – at night. They can see well in the dark and are very sensitive to even the quietest of sounds. But if one is unlucky enough to hop beneath a boa, they are unlikely to get away.

SEE-THROUGH BELLY SKIN HELPS TO BREAK UP THE FROG'S OUTLINE, MAKING IT HARDER TO SPOT

USES HIND LEGS TO KICK OUT AT PREDATORY WASPS

CAMOUFLAGE: SKIN OR FUR MARKINGS THAT HELP AN ANIMAL TO BLEND IN WITH ITS HABITAT

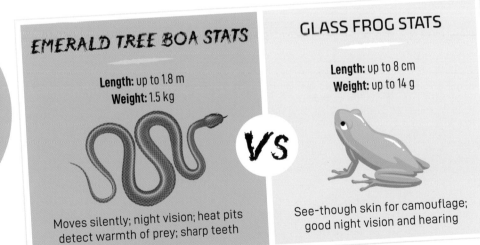

EMERALD TREE BOA STATS

Length: up to 1.8 m
Weight: 1.5 kg

VS

Moves silently; night vision; heat pits detect warmth of prey; sharp teeth

GLASS FROG STATS

Length: up to 8 cm
Weight: up to 14 g

See-though skin for camouflage; good night vision and hearing

VERTICAL PUPILS

Some predatory animals, such as crocodiles and emerald tree boas, have vertical pupils. Scientists think that the ability to squeeze the pupil into a vertical slit helps these animals to judge the distance to their prey with high accuracy.

NILE CROCODILE
vs BLUE WILDEBEEST: JAWS

Nile crocodiles are the apex predators of African rivers. Much of the time they sleep on riverbanks. But when hungry, these giant reptiles will attack and kill pretty much any animal that comes close, including young hippos, elephants and even big cats. An adult Nile crocodile weighs as much as a car and its long, powerful jaws are jammed with more than 60 large teeth.

APEX PREDATOR: THE TOP PREDATOR IN A HABITAT

DEATHLY GRIP

Nile crocodiles are more at home in water than on land. They are good swimmers and often grab fish as they move through the water. With just the top of the croc's eyes, ears and nostrils above the water, animals drinking at the water's edge often don't notice a crocodile's sneaky approach until it's too late. When in range, the croc lunges out of the water and grabs its prey in a deathly grip with powerful jaws. It drowns its victim, batters it against the riverbank or rips chunks off it until it is lifeless.

TAIL FOR SWIMMING AND POWERING ITS HIGH-SPEED LUNGE OUT OF THE WATER

LONG SNOUT WITH ROWS OF POINTED TEETH

HUGE JAW MUSCLES FOR CLAMPING SHUT WITH POWERFUL FORCE

MASSIVE SIZE

CURVED HORNS

LARGE SIZE

BLUE WILDEBEEST

In May and June, more than 1 million of these large grazing mammals migrate north across Tanzania's Serengeti plain in huge herds, searching for greener grass. The most dangerous time for them is when they have to cross the Mara River. As they venture on to the muddy banks, the animals slip and slide – and as they bunch up in the shallows, deadly crocs wait to pounce.

HERDS OFFER GREATER PROTECTION FROM PREDATORS

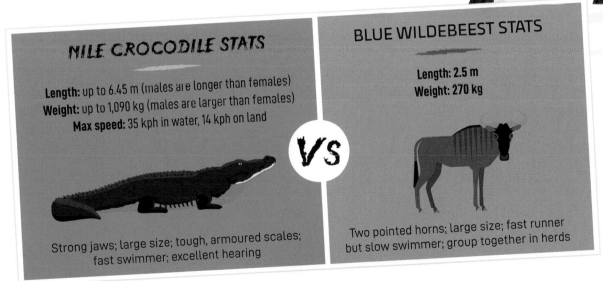

NILE CROCODILE STATS

Length: up to 6.45 m (males are longer than females)
Weight: up to 1,090 kg (males are larger than females)
Max speed: 35 kph in water, 14 kph on land

VS

Strong jaws; large size; tough, armoured scales; fast swimmer; excellent hearing

BLUE WILDEBEEST STATS

Length: 2.5 m
Weight: 270 kg

Two pointed horns; large size; fast runner but slow swimmer; group together in herds

LOCAL KNOWLEDGE

On these long migration journeys across the plains of East Africa the migrating animals have to cross many rivers. Gangs of Nile crocodiles know where the popular crossing places are and lie in wait, ready to pounce on their unsuspecting prey.

GHARIAL
VS MOTTLED EEL: VIBRATIONS

At first sight, this large, fish-eating crocodile looks like log as it floats at the surface of the water. It has a long and very thin snout, which looks more delicate than that of other crocodiles. With more than 100 sharp, interlocking teeth, its snout is ideal for catching and grasping slippery fish. It swallows these whole. Gharials live in rivers, such as the Ganges in India.

AT HOME IN WATER

Gharials are perfectly at home in water, but find it hard to move on land. They come out to bask in the sunshine, especially to warm up in winter. When hunting, a gharial will drive itself through the water by swishing its tail back and forth. Its streamlined shape means it can swim fast underwater. Its snout contains sensory cells that detect the vibrations of swimming fish. By moving its head from side to side, it can pinpoint exactly where the prey is – then grab it.

SNOUT CONTAINS SENSORY CELLS TO DETECT VIBRATIONS

OVER 100 INTERLOCKING TEETH TO HELP TRAP SLIPPERY PREY

EYES AND NOSTRILS ON TOP OF HEAD TO SEE AND BREATHE WHILE LURKING IN WATER

STREAMLINED BODY

INTERLOCK: WHEN TWO THINGS FIT OR LOCK TOGETHER

GHARIALS ARE ONLY FOUND WILD ON THE INDIAN SUBCONTINENT, WHICH INCLUDES THE COUNTRIES OF INDIA, PAKISTAN, BANGLADESH AND SRI LANKA (AMONG OTHERS).

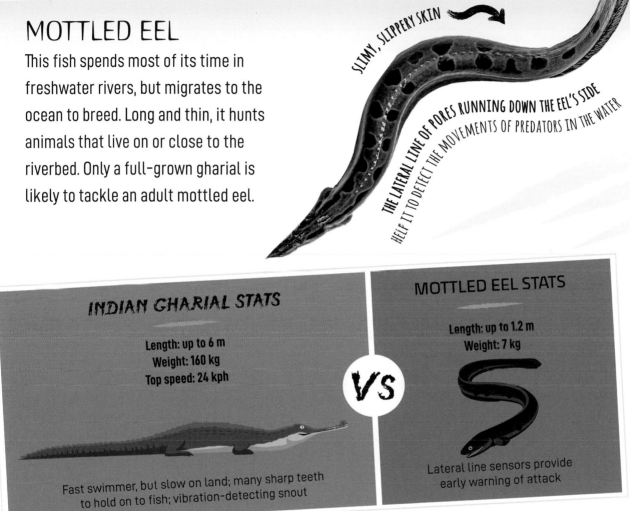

MOTTLED EEL

This fish spends most of its time in freshwater rivers, but migrates to the ocean to breed. Long and thin, it hunts animals that live on or close to the riverbed. Only a full-grown gharial is likely to tackle an adult mottled eel.

SLIMY, SLIPPERY SKIN

THE LATERAL LINE OF PORES RUNNING DOWN THE EEL'S SIDE HELP IT TO DETECT THE MOVEMENTS OF PREDATORS IN THE WATER

INDIAN GHARIAL STATS

Length: up to 6 m
Weight: 160 kg
Top speed: 24 kph

VS

Fast swimmer, but slow on land; many sharp teeth to hold on to fish; vibration-detecting snout

MOTTLED EEL STATS

Length: up to 1.2 m
Weight: 7 kg

Lateral line sensors provide early warning of attack

A SNOUT WITH A 'POT'

Males can be told from females by the pot-shaped lump at the end of their snout. This is called a *ghara*, which is Hindi for 'mud pot'.

KOMODO DRAGON
VS GOAT: POWER

Komodo dragons don't breathe fire, but they are the nearest living thing to mythical dragons. Growing up to three metres long and often weighing close to 100 kilogrammes, they are fearsome predators and the world's biggest reptiles. They have powerful jaws lined with sharp teeth, and wicked claws. Glands in their lower jaw secrete venom, and chemicals called anti-coagulants. When a dragon bites its prey, the anti-coagulants keep its victim's blood from clotting, so it may bleed to death.

SECRETE: WHEN AN ORGAN OR OTHER BODY PART RELEASES LIQUID

BLOODY DEATH

A Komodo dragon lies in wait and leaps out on any animal that passes its hiding place – a goat, deer, snake or even a water buffalo. Dragons are so large and powerful that escape is unlikely. It may rip at its victim's throat, causing the animals to bleed, then bite off chunks of flesh. Often, several dragons join in an attack together. They are the only reptiles to hunt cooperatively like this. They also eat dead animals (carrion).

DEADLY VENOM-DELIVERING JAWS

POWERFUL AND AGGRESSIVE

STRONG CLAWS FOR RIPPING FLESH

MASSIVE BULK

DOMESTICATED GOATS

The only place where Komodo dragons live in the wild is Komodo Island, in Indonesia. People brought domesticated goats to the island for their milk and meat. Many of the goats escaped from captivity and now live in the wild. They make easy prey for the dragons.

SOME SAFETY IN NUMBERS, BUT OTHERWISE DOMESTICATED GOATS ARE POWERLESS AGAINST KOMODO DRAGONS

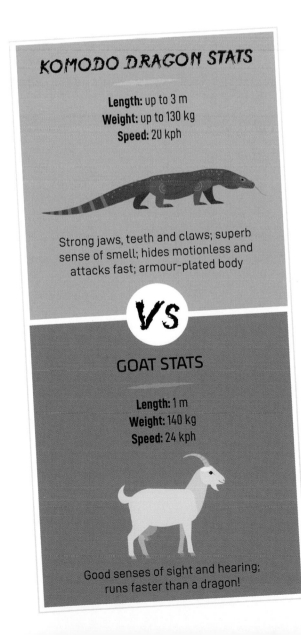

KOMODO DRAGON STATS

Length: up to 3 m
Weight: up to 130 kg
Speed: 20 kph

Strong jaws, teeth and claws; superb sense of smell; hides motionless and attacks fast; armour-plated body

VS

GOAT STATS

Length: 1 m
Weight: 140 kg
Speed: 24 kph

Good senses of sight and hearing; runs faster than a dragon!

MULTI-TALENTED

Komodo dragons can run fast and swim well. Young animals are good at climbing trees. Their sense of hearing is poor and so is their night vision, but their sense of smell is superb.

Like a snake, a Komodo dragon also uses its long, forked tongue and its Jacobson's organ (see page 20) to 'taste' its environment. It can pick up the scent of other animals up to 9 kilometres away.

19

GILA MONSTER
VS DESERT KANGAROO RAT: SMELL

Slow-moving Gila monsters are the biggest lizards in North America. They live in the deserts of Mexico and the southwest US. The deserts are baking hot for much of the year. These lizards use their strong claws to dig cool burrows, where they shelter during the heat of the day.

JACOBSON'S ORGAN

These venomous lizards are much too slow to chase other animals, so most of the time they feed on the eggs of birds and other reptiles. Like many reptiles, a Gila monster often flicks out its tongue to 'taste' the air. Its tongue is so sensitive it can detect eggs a long way off. The Gila monster and other reptiles have a special pit in the roof of the mouth called the Jacobson's organ. As the tongue is flicked out it catches scent particles on it. The particles are then placed inside the Jacobson' organ. This tells the predator the type and location of their intended meal or victim.

CAN STORE FAT IN ITS TAIL AS IT MAY GO FOR MONTHS BETWEEN MEALS

SENSITIVE SENSE OF SMELL

PARTICLE: A TINY PORTION OF MATTER

VENOMOUS JAWS

DESERT KANGAROO RAT

These hopping rodents are fast, and aggressive for their size. They will often drum their hind feet to let predators, such as snakes or Gila monsters, know that they are aware of their presence. They will also kick sand to deter attack. However, a helpless newborn kangaroo rat stands very little chance against the slow advance of a Gila monster.

ALERT SENSES

STRONG BACK LEGS FOR LEAPING, DRUMMING AND KICKING

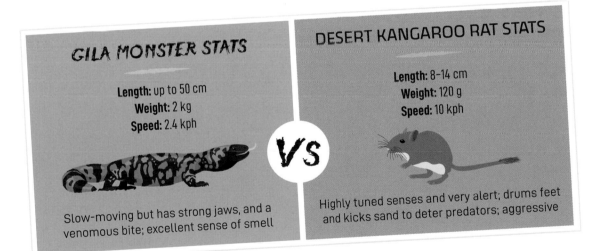

GILA MONSTER STATS

Length: up to 50 cm
Weight: 2 kg
Speed: 2.4 kph

Slow-moving but has strong jaws, and a venomous bite; excellent sense of smell

VS

DESERT KANGAROO RAT STATS

Length: 8–14 cm
Weight: 120 g
Speed: 10 kph

Highly tuned senses and very alert; drums feet and kicks sand to deter predators; aggressive

CHEW AND SWALLOW

If a Gila monster catches a large animal, it chews before swallowing. As it chews, venom from glands in the lower jaw gets into its prey's bloodstream, which weakens the animal. Food can be hard to find in a desert, so if a Gila monster finds a nest with a lot of eggs, it will guzzle the lot. It may not get another meal for a very long time.

FLYING LIZARD
VS TERMITE: AERIAL ATTACK

Flying lizards live in forests in Southeast Asia. They can climb trees with ease and are fast runners. They can also do something that other lizards can't – fly from tree to tree! When one launches itself from a tree, it stretches out flaps of skin on either side of its body, like wings. It has two more wing-like flaps on either side of its head.

SUPER GLIDERS

A flying lizard can't flap these 'wings' like a bird or bat, but they help the animal glide for up to nine metres. So, if it sees a termite or ant nest on a neighbouring tree, it takes the insects by surprise by taking to the air – rather than going the long way round. Once there, the lizard clings to the tree trunk as the insects walk past – and snaffles them up.

Male flying lizards will defend their territories by chasing rival males through the trees in a high-speed aerial pursuit.

GLIDE: TO FLY WITH LITTLE MOVEMENT OF THE WINGS

WING FLAPS ON HEAD

TAIL ACTS LIKE A RUDDER TO HELP STEER IN FLIGHT

SPECIAL LONG RIBS HAVE FOLDS OF SKIN BETWEEN THEM, WHICH WHEN OPENED OUT FORM THE WINGS

TERMITE

Termites are social insects. They live with thousands of others in 'cities' or colonies – mounds of mud or tunnels in tree trunks. When danger approaches, termites release chemicals called pheromones to warn other members of the colony. They can also squirt a foul-tasting liquid at an attacker. This isn't likely to put off a hungry flying lizard, though.

PHEROMONE
WARNING SYSTEM

CAN SQUIRT FOUL LIQUID

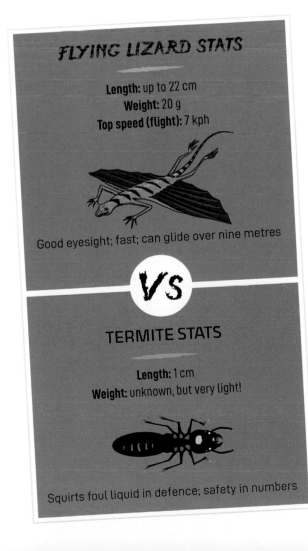

FLYING LIZARD STATS

Length: up to 22 cm
Weight: 20 g
Top speed (flight): 7 kph

Good eyesight; fast; can glide over nine metres

VS

TERMITE STATS

Length: 1 cm
Weight: unknown, but very light!

Squirts foul liquid in defence; safety in numbers

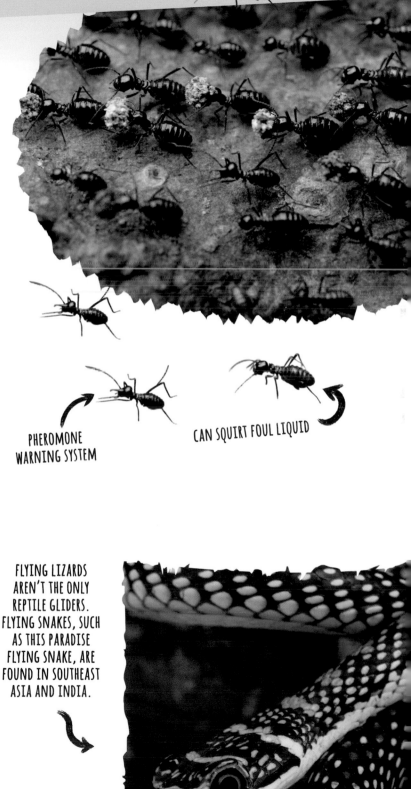

FLYING LIZARDS AREN'T THE ONLY REPTILE GLIDERS. FLYING SNAKES, SUCH AS THIS PARADISE FLYING SNAKE, ARE FOUND IN SOUTHEAST ASIA AND INDIA.

23

BANDED GECKO
VS SCORPION: STALK AND LUNGE

Secretive and nocturnal, this colourful lizard hides from the hot sun under rocks and plants. At night, these predators emerge to hunt baby scorpions, spiders, insects and centipedes in North American deserts. Whereas some lizards are sit-and-wait predators, which means they wait for prey to come to them, banded geckos actively go in search of their next meal.

NOCTURNAL: ACTIVE AT NIGHT

COLOURED AND PATTERNED SKIN TO BLEND IN WITH ITS DESERT HABITAT

EXCELLENT SENSES

CAN SHED ITS TAIL IF GRABBED

CAREFUL APPROACH

When a banded gecko stalks prey, it keeps its eyes fixed on it and slowly walks closer. It holds its body and tail just above the ground and vibrates the tip of its tail. When close enough – it lunges forward and grabs its meal.

A favourite food is baby scorpions, whose sting is still venomous, but the banded gecko is an expert and fast hunter.

ARIZONA BARK SCORPION

Scorpions are desert-living invertebrates with four pairs of jointed legs and a long tail. Their lethal weapon is at the end of the tail – a stinger that injects powerful venom. They use this to kill their own prey – and to defend against predators, such as geckos. The venom of Arizona bark scorpions is strong enough to kill a person – as well as unwary banded geckos.

POWERFUL VENOM DELIVERED BY THE STINGER

PINCERS TO GRAB PREY

TOUGH EXOSKELETON

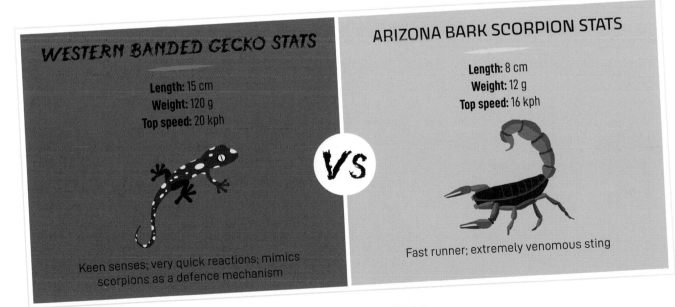

WESTERN BANDED GECKO STATS

Length: 15 cm
Weight: 120 g
Top speed: 20 kph

Keen senses; very quick reactions; mimics scorpions as a defence mechanism

VS

ARIZONA BARK SCORPION STATS

Length: 8 cm
Weight: 12 g
Top speed: 16 kph

Fast runner; extremely venomous sting

PRETEND SCORPIONS

Banded geckos, and some other geckos such as the scorpion-tailed gecko (right), have a trick to warn off predators. They curl their tail above their back and wave it around so they look like as a scorpion – that's enough to put off some enemies.

SNAPPING TURTLE VS AMERICAN ALLIGATOR: SNAPPING JAWS

An alligator snapping turtle is a North American freshwater reptile that stays hidden most of the time. Its mud-coloured, spiky shell gives it good camouflage in a murky river. It can stay underwater for almost an hour at a time before having to come to the surface to breathe.

A WAITING GAME

Most of the time, a 'snapper' doesn't do very much. It remains almost motionless in the mud on the bottom of its slow-flowing river with its huge mouth wide open. Only one part of its body moves – the long, pink 'finger' on the end of its tongue. It wiggles this like a worm.

When a fish sees the 'worm', it comes close, thinking the worm will make a nice meal. Then, snap! The turtle closes its ultra-strong jaws and there's no escape for its prey. Snapping turtles eat anything that can fit in their jaws. As well as fish, they eat frogs, ducks, snakes, other turtles and even young alligators!

MOTIONLESS: NOT MOVING

NAMED FOR THE ALLIGATOR SKIN-LIKE RIDGES ON ITS SHELL

CAN STAY UNDERWATER FOR UP TO AN HOUR

WORM-LIKE TONGUE FOR LURING PREY

FEROCIOUSLY SHARP, BEAK-LIKE MOUTH

EYES AND NOSTRILS ON THE TOP OF THE HEAD

SNAP: TO SHUT VERY QUICKLY

POWERFUL SNAPPING JAWS

BODY AND TAIL DESIGNED FOR SWIMMING

AMERICAN ALLIGATOR

Alligators are also top predators and can grow very large. There's no way a snapping turtle will attack one that's fully grown. But alligators start out small. A young one, less than a metre long, will make a good meal for a snapper. American alligators are very protective of their young, so an alligator snapper will have to approach with caution ...

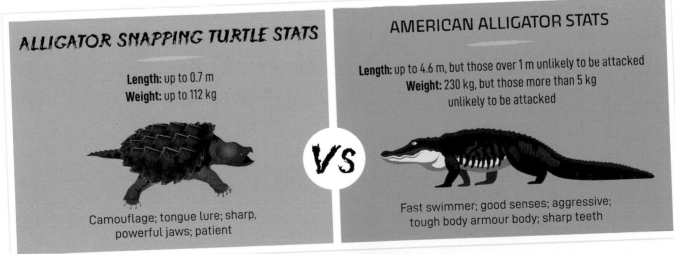

ALLIGATOR SNAPPING TURTLE STATS

Length: up to 0.7 m
Weight: up to 112 kg

Camouflage; tongue lure; sharp, powerful jaws; patient

VS

AMERICAN ALLIGATOR STATS

Length: up to 4.6 m, but those over 1 m unlikely to be attacked
Weight: 230 kg, but those more than 5 kg unlikely to be attacked

Fast swimmer; good senses; aggressive; tough body armour body; sharp teeth

HOW OLD?

Alligator snappers grow throughout their lives. Some live to be well over 100 years old, by which time they may weigh 100 kilogrammes or more.

LOGGERHEAD TURTLE
vs HORSESHOE CRAB:
CRUSHING AND GRINDING JAWS

The loggerhead turtle is the world's second-largest sea turtle — only the giant leatherback turtle is bigger. Loggerheads live in warm waters in parts of the Atlantic, Indian and Pacific Oceans. Loggerheads are graceful swimmers, using their flippers to gently navigate around coral reefs as they look for food. They can dive 300 metres below the surface and stay underwater for several hours before having to come up for air.

PROTECTIVE SHELL

Loggerheads' large size and tough shell means few other animals will attack them, and they are predators themselves. They often hunt venomous jellyfish. The turtle's shell protects it from the jellyfish's stinging tentacles. These turtles also eat shellfish, lobsters, starfish, sea urchins, and crabs on the seabed and fish swimming above. Even horseshoe crabs, with their tough exoskeleton are no problem for this turtle. Loggerheads crush prey with their large, grinding jaws.

HARD SHELL

POWERFUL JAW MUSCLES IN BOTH CHEEKS (BEHIND EACH EYE)

STRONG BEAK-LIKE JAWS

LOGGERHEADS CAN USE THEIR FRONT FLIPPERS TO MOVE FOOD INTO POSITION BEFORE THEY SWALLOW IT.

28

GRIND: TO CRUSH OR RUB SOMETHING INTO SMALLER PIECES

HARD EXOSKELETON
COVERS THE WHOLE BODY AND HEAD

CAN USE ITS TAIL TO
RIGHT ITSELF
IF IT IS FLIPPED OVER
BY A PREDATOR

HORSESHOE CRAB

Horseshoe crabs have been called 'living fossils' because they originated around 450 million years ago. They are strange-looking creatures that spend most of their time swimming close to the seabed in search of their next meal – shellfish and worms. They are not true crabs at all, but members of a group of animals called chelicerates and are related to spiders. These creatures have a tough exoskeleton and a long tail.

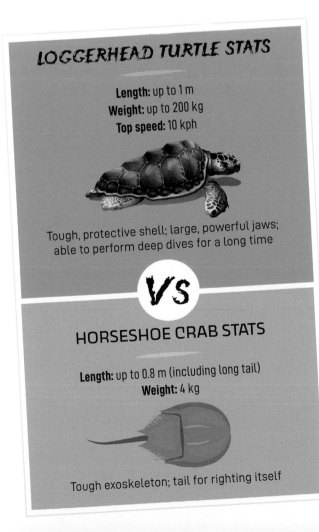

LOGGERHEAD TURTLE STATS

Length: up to 1 m
Weight: up to 200 kg
Top speed: 10 kph

Tough, protective shell; large, powerful jaws; able to perform deep dives for a long time

VS

HORSESHOE CRAB STATS

Length: up to 0.8 m (including long tail)
Weight: 4 kg

Tough exoskeleton; tail for righting itself

EXOSKELETON:
HARD OUTER SHELL-LIKE COVERING FOUND ON MANY INVERTEBRATES

PORTUGUESE MAN-O'-WAR JELLYFISH ARE A FAVOURITE FOOD OF LOGGERHEADS. BUT THE TURTLES DON'T GET STUNG BY THE DEADLY JELLYFISH VENOM BECAUSE THE SKIN THAT LINES THE TURTLE'S MOUTH AND THROAT IS SO TOUGH.

GLOSSARY

agile able to move quickly and easily

camouflage fur or skin markings that help an animal to hide in its habitat

carnivore an animal that eats only meat

cartilage a firm, flexible connective tissue found in parts of the body

clot when blood has thickened and become solid or semi-solid

colony a group of animals of the same species that live together; the physical structure that they live in

cooperatively working towards a common goal

coral reef a hard ridge in the sea made of coral – a stony substance made from the skeletons of tiny sea animals

exoskeleton hard cover of an invertebrate's body – especially spiders, insects and crustaceans

forage to search widely for food

glands organs in the body that secrete chemicals

habitat the natural home of a plant or animal

herbivore an animal that eats only plants

invertebrate an animal without a backbone; spiders, insects, snails and jellyfish are all invertebrates

mammal a warm-blooded animal with a backbone and that has hair or fur at some stage in its life and is fed on its mother's milk when young

migrate to move from one place to another according to the seasons

navigate to find the way

organ a body part with a specific function, such as the heart or liver

pheromones chemicals produced and released by some animals that affect the behaviour of other animals of the same species

predator an animal that hunts and kills other animals for food

prey/prey on an animal that is hunted for food (noun); to hunt and kill for food (verb)

reptile an animal with scaly skin, whose body temperature is the same as the environment around it. Reptiles may bask in the sun to warm up or seek shade to cool down

rodent a mammal whose front teeth (incisors) grow all the time and must gnaw constantly to wear them down; rats, squirrels and capybara are all rodents

scales horny or bony plates that may overlap and that protect the skin of many fish and reptiles

social living together in an organised community

submerge to cover with water

suffocate to kill by cutting off a prey animal's air supply, so it can't breathe

thrive to live or develop well

toxic describes something that is poisonous

FURTHER INFORMATION

BOOKS

Animal Tongues / Animal Tails
by Tim Harris (Wayland, 2019)

Animals in Disguise
by Michael Bright (Wayland, 2020)

Visual Explorers: Predators
by Toby Reynolds and Paul Calver (Franklin Watts, 2015)

Wildlife Worlds (series)
by Tim Harris (Franklin Watts, 2020)

WEBSITES

Check out the BBC bitesize website for lots of information relevant to this book and information on food chains.
www.bbc.co.uk/bitesize/topics/zx882hv/articles/z3c2xnb

The website addresses (URLs) in this book were valid at the time of going to press. However, it is possible that the contents or addresses may have changed since the publication of this book. No responsibility for any such changes can be accepted by either the author or the Publisher. We strongly advise that Internet access is supervised by a responsible adult.

National Geographic gives good introductions to the lifestyles of a range of mammals. These are some of the best pages.

Anaconda: **www.kids.nationalgeographic.com/animals/reptiles/anaconda/**
Emerald tree boa: **www.nationalgeographic.org/projects/photo-ark/animal/corallus-caninus/**
Flying lizard: **www.nationalgeographic.com/animals/reptiles/d/draco-lizard/**
Gharial: **www.nationalgeographic.com/animals/reptiles/g/gharial/**
Gila monster: **www.kids.nationalgeographic.com/animals/reptiles/gila-monster/**
King cobra: **www.kids.nationalgeographic.com/animals/reptiles/king-cobra/**
Komodo dragon: **www.nationalgeographic.com/animals/reptiles/k/komodo-dragon/**
Loggerhead turtle: **www. kids.nationalgeographic.com/animals/reptiles/loggerhead-sea-turtle/**
Nile crocodile: **www.kids.nationalgeographic.com/animals/reptiles/nile-crocodile/**
Snapping turtle: **www.nationalgeographic.com/animals/reptiles/a/alligator-snapping-turtle/**

INDEX